THE

Name Game

OR

"Paging Mr. Catrazz…Mr. Al Catrazz…"

THE
Name Game

OR

"Paging Mr. Catrazz...Mr. Al Catrazz..."

SUE DONYM

as told to
Jon Korkes, B.S.
Deena Silver-Kramer, F.N.E.
Dr. Howard Orenstein
Dr. Norman Stiles
and
Pete Abread

POCKET BOOKS
New York   London   Toronto   Sydney   Tokyo   Singapore

This book is a work of fiction. Names, characters, places and incidents are products of the author's imagination or are used fictitiously. And resemblance to actual events or locales or persons, living or dead, is entirely coincidental.

An *Original* Publication of POCKET BOOKS

POCKET BOOKS, a division of Simon & Schuster Inc.
1230 Avenue of the Americas, New York, NY 10020

Copyright © 1994 by Peter Gethers, Norman Stiles, Jon Korkes, Howard Orenstein and Deena Kramer

Library of Congress Cataloging-in-Publication Number: 94-67393

ISBN: 0-671-89951-1

First Pocket Books trade paperback printing October 1994

10 9 8 7 6 5 4 3 2 1

POCKET and colophon are registered trademarks of Simon & Schuster Inc.

Cover design by Matthew Galemmo
Cover art by David Goldin
Text design by Stanley S. Drate/Folio Graphics Co., Inc.

Printed in the U.S.A.

Introduction

It all began with Jośe Canyousee.

After that, brave and visionary pioneers working in the underappreciated field of punology risked ostracism and ridicule when they announced to a semicomatose world their startling discovery of Mr. Izzy Naked and Mr. Dick Hertz.

And now, years and many sleepless nights later, the official version of the **Name Game** has been born, building on this early scholarly work and taking it to a new and *much* more annoying level.

Here's how to play the **Name Game:**

Start with a word like "aluminum." Note that the first syllable is "al," as in the common first name "Al." The rest of the word is the not-so-common surname "Uminum." If you write it out phonetically, which makes it a little easier to pronounce when coming upon it cold, you now have a person by the name of "Al Oominum." If you want to take it a step further, you might be interested in meeting his cousin Mr. Al Oominumfoil, a very successful professional sandwich-wrapper. Go ahead and try it with the word "microphone" or "testicle." You should get the idea. If you don't, what are you doing buying a book? You should be home watching TV, trying to figure out the deeper meaning of *Married . . . With Children*.

While playing the **Name Game,** we discovered that it's a lot more fun—and a lot harder to guess the entire name—when the last name is said first. And, for some reason, it's particularly hysterical when you set up things with a "page." We like the idea of customers in a cigar store hearing "Paging Mr. Madoar . . . Mr. Hugh Madoar." Or, in a Middle Eastern restaurant, diners listening to someone say: "Paging Mr. Tillsoup

. . . Mr. Len Tillsoup." So, that's the way we've set up most of the names in this book. If you're looking for Mr. Wade Ingroom, you'll find him being paged in a hospital. If you're searching for Mr. Al Coholick, you'll probably hear him paged at the Betty Ford Clinic.

The **Name Game** can be played by anyone, anywhere, at any time. You can play it while you dine outdoors (just ask Mr. Fresco . . . Mr. Al Fresco) or while you're in a garden (check it out with Ms. Gold . . . Mrs. Mary Gold). You don't have to be rich (confirmed by the hardworking Ms. Torr . . . Ms. Janet Torr) or popular (if you can find him, ask Mr. Ittaire . . . Mr. Sol Ittaire) or even sane (speak to Ms. Neeyack . . . Ms. Mae Neeyack).

The Name Game does not contain, by any means, a definitive list of names or categories. We know that there is no end to the possibilities, but we reached the end of our rope. One more day of list making and we'd be checking into the Bates Motel, sharing a room with Mr. Kottick . . . Mr. Sy Kottick.

Now it's up to you. The future of the **Name Game** is in your hands. Just be careful. This does tend to be addictive. So, when you wake up at three in the morning, turn on the light, poke your snoring spouse, and say, "I've got it! Paging Mr. Antsleep . . . Mr. Ike Antsleep," don't say we didn't warn you.

1 Paging:

Mr. Nappattee . . . Mr. Bo Nappattee

People Likely to Be Paged:

AT AN ITALIAN RESTAURANT

Mr. Zapie	Mr. Pete Zapie
Mr. Aronee	Mr. Mack Aronee
Mr. Balls	Mr. Meade Balls
Ms. Tipasto	Ms. Ann Tipasto
Mr. Amari	Mr. Cal Amari
Ms. Gwini	Ms. Lynn Gwini
Mr. Cottee	Mr. Manny Cottee
Mr. Lee	Mr. Zeppo Lee

Mr. Zone .... Mr. Cal Zone
Ms. Stronee .... Ms. Minnie Stronee
Mr. Timbohka .... Mr. Sol Timbohka
Mr. Fresco .... Mr. Al Fresco
Mr. Resco .... Mr. Alf Resco

AT AN ITALIAN RESTAURANT IN NEW DELHI
Mr. Olee .... Mr. Ravi Olee
Ms. Miatable .... Ms. Gita Miatable
Ms. Meemifood .... Ms. Gita Meemifood

AT A FRENCH RESTAURANT
Ms. Tradee .... Ms. May Tradee
Mr. Lomadam .... Mr. Al Lomadam
Mr. Lomonsieur .... Mr. Al Lomonsieur
Ms. Sheff .... Ms. Sue Sheff
Mr. Vooplait .... Mr. Syl Vooplait
Mr. Grett .... Mr. Vinnie Grett
Ms. D'Foisgras .... Ms. Pattie D'Foisgras

Mr. Goh .... Mr. Oscar Goh
Mr. Brulay .... Mr. Kareem Brulay
Ms. Tass .... Ms. Demi Tass
Mr. Littlebreezeseemstowhisperlouise . . .
          Mr. Avery Littlebreezeseemstowhisperlouise

AT A SEAFOOD RESTAURANT
Mr. Fish .... Mr. Shel Fish
Mr. Chowder .... Mr. Clem Chowder
Mr. Ensole .... Mr. Lem Ensole
Mr. Ibutt .... Mr. Hal Ibutt
Mr. Erill .... Mr. Mack Erill

AT A CHINESE RESTAURANT
Mr. Outemessjee .... Mr. Whit Outemessjee
Ms. Lingricesoup .... Ms. "Sis" Lingricesoup
Mr. Peeduck .... Mr. Chris Peeduck
Mr. Shoopork .... Mr. Moe Shoopork
Mr. Cheenutz .... Mr. Lee Cheenutz

3

AT A CHINESE RESTAURANT IN ACAPULCO
Mr. Tonsoup .... Mr. Juan Tonsoup
Mr. Fromcolumay .... Mr. Juan Fromcolumay

AT A CHINESE RESTAURANT IN MOSCOW
Ms. Wanchicken .... Ms. Sasha Wanchicken

AT A JAPANESE RESTAURANT
Ms. Moovyoorshooz .... Ms. Rhea Moovyoorshooz
Ms. Fornyaroll .... Ms. Callie Fornyaroll
Ms. Shee .... Ms. Sue Shee
Mr. Akisauce .... Mr. Terry Akisauce

AT A MEXICAN RESTAURANT
Mr. Dooweeyeet .... Mr. Juan Dooweeyeet
Ms. Chillotta .... Ms. Ann Chillotta
Mr. Appeenya .... Mr. Hal Appeenya
Ms. Frydebeanz .... Ms. Rhea Frydebeanz
Ms. Heetah .... Ms. Fay Heetah

AT A GREEK RESTAURANT

Ms. Tahcheez .... Ms. Fay Tacheez

AT A MIDDLE EASTERN RESTAURANT

Mr. Tillsoup .... Mr. Len Tillsoup

Mr. Odough .... Mr. Phil Odough

Mr. Saka .... Mr. Moe Saka

Mr. Abread .... Mr. Pete Abread

Mr. Ganousch .... Mr. Bubba Ganoush

Mr. Peeze .... Mr. Chick Peeze

AT AN INDIAN RESTAURANT

Mr. Foryoursupper .... Mr. Singh Foryoursupper

Mr. Nuss .... Mr. Ravi Nuss

Mr. Encurry .... Mr. Chick Encurry

Mr. Hatmaghandi .... Mr. Moe Hatmaghandi

AT A SOUL FOOD RESTAURANT

Ms. Izmywomannow .... Ms. Bess U. Izmywomannow

Mr. Greensplease .... Mr. Moe Greensplease

AT A DELI

Mr. Zaball .... Mr. Matt Zaball

Mr. Lonee .... Mr. Beau Lonee

Ms. Filtafish .... Ms. Gay Filtafish

Mr. Slaw .... Mr. Cole Slaw

Mr. Sanbeenz .... Mr. Frank Sanbeenz

Ms. Cornebeef .... Ms. Leena Cornebeef

Mr. Ahmee .... Mr. Sal Ahmee

Mr. Onrye .... Mr. Ham Onrye

Mr. Gazzunt .... Mr. Sy Gazzunt

AT A DELI IN NEW DELHI

Mr. Veeyeet .... Mr. Vindu Veeyeet

AT THE DINER

Ms. Elltee	Ms. Bea Elltee
Mr. Indressing	Mr. Rush Indressing
Mr. Lomode	Mr. Al Lomode
Ms. Rolle	Ms. Cassie Rolle
Mr. Orfsalad	Mr. Walt Orfsalad
Mr. Cornishen	Mr. Rock Cornishen
Ms. Nuttbutter	Ms. Pia Nuttbutter
Mr. Nillapudding	Mr. Van Nillapudding
Mr. Tedmilk	Mr. Mal Tedmilk
Ms. Pulsyrup	Ms. Mae Pulsyrup
Mr. Rowave	Mr. Mike Rowave
Mr. Tress	Mr. Wade Tress
Mr. Tinpepper	Mr. Saul Tinpepper

AT A STEAK HOUSE

Ms. Sklub	Ms. Dinah Sklub
Mr. Anpotatoes	Mr. Meade Anpotatoes
Mr. Roast	Mr. Chuck Roast
Ms. Fwellington	Ms. Bea Fwellington
Mr. Minyun	Mr. Phillie Minyun
Mr. Monico	Mr. Del Monico
Mr. Steak	Mr. Shel Steak
Ms. Tedpotatoes	Ms. Rose Tedpotatoes
Mr. Aisesauce	Mr. Bern Aisesauce
Mr. Iumrayer	Mr. Meade Iumrayer

AT A WINE STEWARD'S CONVENTION

Mr. Yard	Mr. Vin Yard
Mr. Ling	Mr. Reese Ling
Mr. Whine	Mr. Wyatt Whine
Mr. Whine	Mr. Rhett Whine
Mr. Pollichella	Mr. Val Pollichella
Mr. Ernay	Mr. Cab Ernay

Mr. Foussay .... Mr. Paulie Foussay
Ms. Ette .... Ms. Claire Ette

AT THE CORNER BAR

Mr. Ender .... Mr. Bart Ender
Mr. Auer .... Mr. Hap E. Auer
Ms. Ridge .... Ms. Bev Ridge
Ms. Uptothebarr .... Ms. Belle E. Uptothebarr
Mr. Kerr .... Mr. Lee Kerr
Mr. Ball .... Mr. Hy Ball
Mr. Skee .... Mr. Bruce Skee
Mr. Weiser .... Mr. Budd Weiser
Mr. Earplease .... Mr. Abe Earplease
Mr. Zelittdown .... Mr. Gus Zelittdown
Ms. Waitressover .... Ms. Cindy Waitressover
Mr. Moreforyou .... Mr. Noah Moreforyou
Mr. Chandsoda .... Mr. Scott Chandsoda
Mr. Yay .... Mr. Perry Yay
Mr. Istoga .... Mr. Cal Istoga

Mr. Knee .... Mr. Marty Knee
Mr. Vados .... Mr. Cal Vados
Ms. Zette .... Ms. Anna Zette
Mr. Nail .... Mr. Russ T. Nail
Ms. Eontherocks .... Ms. Martine Eontherocks
Ms. Skeenocherry .... Ms. Mara Skeenocherry
Ms. Snifter .... Ms. Brandy Snifter
Mr. Perr .... Mr. Stu Perr
Mr. Wonon .... Mr. Ty Wonon
Mr. Gnateddriver .... Mr. Desi Gnateddriver

AT THE GREENGROCER

Ms. Antro .... Ms. Ceil Antro
Mr. O'Lee .... Mr. Brock O'Lee
Mr. Dickeeo .... Mr. Ray Dickeeo
Mr. Bayga .... Mr. Rudy Bayga
Mr. Choke .... Mr. Artie Choke
Mr. Aydo .... Mr. Tom Aydo

AT THE CANDY COUNTER

Mr. Zanettes .... Mr. Ray Zanettes

Mr. Ulls .... Mr. Chuck Ulls

Ms. Nuttbrittle .... Ms. Pia Nuttbrittle

Mr. Monjoy .... Mr. Al Monjoy

Mr. Barr .... Mr. Clark Barr

Mr. Corish .... Mr. Lee Corish

AT THE HEALTH FOOD STORE

Mr. Falfa .... Mr. Al Falfa

Mr. Alfa .... Mr. Alf Alfa

Ms. Hipps .... Ms. Rose Hipps

Ms. Ralwater .... Ms. Minnie Ralwater

Mr. Ull .... Mr. Herb Ull

Mr. Minz .... Mr. Vida Minz

2 Paging:

Ms. Zhuretyme . . .
Ms. Leigh Zhuretyme

People Likely to Be Paged:

AT A VIDEO STORE

Mr. Izzencane	Mr. Sid Izzencane
Mr. Lone	Mr. Homer Lone
Mr. Encounters	Mr. Klaus Encounters
Ms. Sell	Ms. Cara Sell
Ms. Immelcrackers	Ms. Ann Immelcrackers
Ms. Zuvsaintmareeze	Ms. Belle Zuvsaintmareeze

Mr. Thalweppin .... Mr. Lee Thalweppin
Ms. Dayinn .... Ms. Holly Dayinn
Ms. Fantman .... Ms. Ella Fantman
Ms. Nerr .... Ms. Di Nerr
Mr. Iverence .... Mr. Del Iverence
Mr. Ridgetoofarr .... Mr. Abe Ridgetoofarr
Ms. Thonman .... Ms. Mara Thonman
Mr. Hooztalking .... Mr. Luke Hooztalking
Ms. Ottsuvfire .... Ms. Sherry Ottsuvfire
Mr. Betterblues .... Mr. Moe Betterblues
Mr. Adelfeeya .... Mr. Phil Adelfeeya
Ms. Vanayshun .... Ms. Bertha Vanayshun
Mr. Toolive .... Mr. Ivan Toolive
Mr. Oweenparthree .... Mr. Hal Oweenpartthree
Mr. Ahalf .... Mr. Aiden Ahalf
Mr. Sizzwithwolves .... Mr. Dan Sizzwithwolves
Mr. Jingbull .... Mr. Ray Jingbull
Mr. Lenceofthelambs ...... Mr. Sy Lenceofthelambs
Mr. Rassickpark .... Mr. Joe Rassickpark

AT A SWEDISH VIDEO STORE

Mr. Yesterday .... Mr. Bjorn Yesterday

AT THE THEATER

Mr. Sydestoree .... Mr. Wes Sydestoree
Mr. Treetcarnamadesire .... Mr. "Ace" Treetcarnamedesire
Mr. Torialdaybue .... Mr. Derek Torialdaybue
Ms. Tagonist .... Ms. Ann Tagonist
Ms. Hindthaseenze .... Ms. Bea Hindthaseenze
Ms. Dinglady .... Ms. Lee Dinglady
Mr. Dingman .... Mr. Lee Dingman
Ms. Hearse .... Ms. Rhea Hearse
Mr. Vreeview .... Mr. Ray Vreeview
Mr. Orrnottoobee .... Mr. Toby Orrnottoobee

AT AN ISRAELI PRODUCTION OF *THE KING AND I*

Mr. Siamezeiffyoopleeze ... Mr. Chaim Siamezeiffyoopleeze

AT A HOLLYWOOD MOVIE STUDIO

Mr. Maker .... Mr. Phil Maker
Mr. O'deal .... Mr. Stu D. O'deal
Mr. Meditor .... Mr. Phil Meditor
Mr. Ingstarr .... Mr. Bud Ingstarr
Mr. Hanger .... Mr. Cliff Hanger
Mr. Uloid .... Mr. Sal Uloid
Mr. Ebrity .... Mr. Saul Ebrity
Mr. Key .... Mr. Mark Key
Ms. Wright .... Ms. Rhea Wright
Mr. Shireboulevard .... Mr. Will Shireboulevard

AT A CZECHOSLOVAKIAN MOVIE STUDIO

Mr. Unch .... Mr. Havel Unch

AT THE ACADEMY AWARDS

Ms. Ihavetheenvelopeplease Ms. May Ihavetheenvelopeplease
Ms. Thewinnerrizz .... Ms. Ann Thewinnerrizz
Ms. Thankeverybody .... Ms. Ivana Thankeverybody

Ms. Rector .... Ms. Bess D. Rector
Mr. Tor .... Mr. Eddy Tor
Ms. Kupplaydee .... Ms. Mae Kupplaydee
Mr. Likemeyooreallylikeme Mr. Hugh
                                     Likemeyooreallylikeme

AT THE EMMY AWARDS

Ms. Aylaw .... Ms. Elle Aylaw
Ms. Moonerz .... Ms. Honey Moonerz
Mr. Betyourlife .... Mr. Hugh Betyourlife
Mr. Deryeers .... Mr. Juan Deryeers
Mr. Tassyisland .... Mr. Van Tassyisland
Mr. Woodtonite .... Mr. Vern Woodtonite
Ms. Ningshade .... Mr. Eve Ningshade
Ms. Teenest .... Ms. Em Teenest
Mr. Aboutchoo .... Mr. Matt Aboutchoo
Mr. Dafammillee .... Mr. Alan Defammillee

AT A CHILDREN'S TV SHOW

Mr. Eeseaze	Mr. Abe Eeseaze
Mr. Bett	Mr. Alfie Bett
Mr. Cookiemonster	Mr. Hymie Cookiemonster

ON THE SET OF *GET SMART*

Mr. Beeleeve	Mr. Woody Hugh Beeleeve
Ms. Oss	Ms. Kay Oss

AT A CLINT EASTWOOD FILM FESTIVAL

Ms. Kmyday	Ms. May Kmyday

AT THE WALT DISNEY STUDIO EXECUTIVE OFFICES

Ms. Mayshun	Ms. Anna Mayshun
Mr. Eemouse	Mr. Mick Eemouse
Mr. Elduck	Mr. Don Elduck
Ms. Lox	Ms. Goldie Lox
Ms. Rella	Ms. Cindy Rella
Ms. Fofumm	Ms. Fifi Fofumm

Ms. Nevaland .... Ms. Neva Nevaland
Mr. Derland .... Mr. Juan Derland
Mr. Ellengrettle .... Mr. Hans Ellengrettle

AT A PORN FILM CASTING CALL

Ms. Vershot .... Ms. Bea Vershot
Ms. Lingus .... Ms. Connie Lingus
Mr. D'andlassivious .... Mr. Lou D'andlassivious
Mr. Indahay .... Mr. Erroll Indahay
Mr. Uvyoo .... Mr. Seymour Uvyoo
Mr. Wayouwannitt .... Mr. Henry Wayouwannitt
Mr. Pendous .... Mr. Stu Pendous
Mr. Brication .... Mr. Lou Brication
Ms. Over .... Ms. Eileen Over
Ms. Nem .... Ms. Essie Nem

AT THE CIRCUS

My Eyekle .... Ms. Eunice Eyekle
Mr. Gerr .... Mr. Ty Gerr

Ms. Leeclown .... Ms. Syl Leeclown
Ms. Dextrous .... Ms. Amber Dextrous
Mr. Ameeztwinz .... Mr. Sy Ammeeztwinz
Ms. Graytizzshowonearth .. Ms. Dee Graytizzshowonearth

Big-Top Bulletin

Daredevils Hy Wire and Ty Tropewalker announced today they will no longer be performing with longtime partner "Ace" Ayfteenette. "The act needs new blood," Mr. Tropewalker said. "That's why we're adding the exciting team of 'Dizzy' Spells and Luke Outbelow."

Mr. Ayfteenette announced, "From now on, I'm going to work with people who need and appreciate me, like Lee Poffaroof. I even have an offer to go to Japan and work with Les Q. Ninewunnwunn."

The owner of the Big Top Show, Sir Cussmogull, could not be reached for comment.

People Likely to Be Paged:

AT A BEATLES CONCERT

Ms. Holdyerhand .... Ms. Ivana Holdyerhand
Mr. Terrday .... Mr. Jess Terrday
Ms. Errpool .... Ms. Liv Errpool
Ms. Tulls .... Ms. Bea Tulls
Ms. Vzmeeyehyehyeh ...... Ms. Sheila Vzmeeyehyehyeh

AT A STONES CONCERT

Mr. Antgetnosatisfaction ... Mr. Ike Antgetnosatisfaction

AT A DYLAN CONCERT

Mr. Waysixtywun .... Mr. Hy Waysixtywun

AT A PEARL JAM CONCERT

Mr. Ufforya .... Mr. Loudon Ufforya
Ms. Tingwontoothreefore .. Ms. Tess Tingwontoothreefore

Mr. Deer .... Mr. Pierce Deer
Mr. Tongue .... Mr. Pierce Tongue

AT A STEVIE WONDER CONCERT
Mr. Ufforthesihtee .... Mr. Justin Ufforthesihtee
Ms. Perrstishun .... Ms. Sue Perstishun

AT A SPRINGSTEEN CONCERT
Mr. Indayooessay .... Mr. Bjorn Indayooessay

AT WOODSTOCK
Mr. Dee .... Mr. Ellis Dee
Mr. Oosinojen .... Mr. Hal Oosinojen
Ms. Wanna .... Ms. Mary Wanna
Mr. Cupulkogold .... Mr. Al Cupulkogold
Ms. Nah .... Ms. Shana Nah
Ms. Kluvnotwarr .... Ms. Mae Kluvnotwarr
Ms. Bottoms .... Ms. Belle Bottoms

Mr. Paper .... Mr. Roland Paper
Mr. Ellbagg .... Mr. Nick Ellbagg
Ms. Ellnewyork .... Ms. Beth Ellnewyork
Mr. Iffornyadreamin .... Mr. Kal Iffornyadreamin

AT A WOODSTOCK REUNION

Mr. Yularphone .... Mr. Sal Yularphone
Ms. Kaff .... Ms. Dee Kaff
Ms. Ellbean .... Ms. Elle Ellbean
Ms. Bocks .... Ms. Rhea Bocks
Ms. Lox .... Ms. May Lox
Ms. Tassid .... Ms. Ann Tassid
Mr. Trinn .... Mr. Moe Trinn
Mr. Colesterall .... Mr. Hy Colesterall
Ms. Emdubbelyoo .... Ms. Bea Emdubbelyoo
Mr. Uss .... Mr. Lex Uss
Mr. Anjackett .... Mr. Ty Anjackett
Ms. Slift .... Ms. Fay Slift
Mr. Ceedinghairline .... Mr. Rhea Ceedinghairline

Mr. Tunns .... Mr. Ham Tunns
Ms. Itchconetakit .... Ms. Gwen Itchconetakit
Mr. Port .... Mr. Wes Port

AT A SINATRA CONCERT

Ms. Mannuhvdaboard ..... Ms. Cher Mannuhvdaboard
Mr. Dingding .... Mr. Ringo Dingding
Ms. Way .... Ms. Maya Way
Ms. Kyndatown .... Ms. Maya Kyndatown

AT A DON HO CONCERT

Mr. Kahlaylee .... Mr. Hugh Kahlaylee

AT CARNEGIE HALL

Ms. Olinsection .... Ms. Vy Olinsection
Ms. Nett .... Ms. Clara Nett
Ms. O'Solo .... Ms. P. Ann O'Solo
Mr. Brow .... Mr. Hy Brow
Mr. Orianchant .... Mr. Greg Orianchant

Mr. Ize .... Mr. Harmon Ize

Mr. Zophone .... Mr. Zack Zophone

Ms. Sharp .... Ms. Dee Sharp

Ms. Flatt .... Ms. Dee Flatt

Mr. Eggro .... Mr. Al Eggro

Mr. Note .... Mr. Hy Note

Mr. Tonesax .... Mr. Barry Tonesax

Ms. Ershopquartette .... Ms. Barb Ershopquartette

Mr. Ah .... Mr. Ari Ah

Ms. Olin .... Ms. Vi Olin

Mr. Tosax .... Mr. Al Tosax

IN THE ASCAP LOBBY

Mr. Meebacktowolevirginny . . .

Mr. Cary Meebacktowolevirginny

Mr. Lookingoveraforleefclover . . .

Mr. Chaim Lookingoveraforleefclover

Mr. Ingsinngloccamorra .... Mr. Howard Ingsinngloccamorra

Mr. Singmatilda .... Mr. Walt Singmatilda

Mr. Ounyerrockindaboat .. Mr. Sid Ownyerrockindaboat
Mr. Youizorizyouaintmybaby ...

Mr. Iz Youizorizyouaintmybaby
Ms. Stickatedladee .... Ms. Sophie Stickatedladee
Ms. Moonhitzyereyelikeabigpizzapie ...

Mrs. Wendy Moonhitzyereyelikeabigpizzapie

IN THE STOCKHOLM ASCAP LOBBY
Ms. Melankollybaybee ..... Ms. Mai Melankollybaybee

IN THE PALESTINIAN ASCAP LOBBY
Ms. Sheezmabaybee .... Mr. Yasser Sheezmabaybee
Mr. Idontmeanmaybee ..... Mr. Nosair Idontmeanmaybee
Mr. Himmonnsonday ...... Mr. Ahmet Himmonnsonday

AT GRACELAND
Mr. Daburns .... Mr. Sy Daburns
Mr. Ayntnuttenbuttahowndogg ...

Mr. Hugh Ayntnuttenbuttahowndogg

Mr. Brakehotell	Mr. Art Brakehotell
Mr. Stillalive	Mr. Izzy Stillalive
Ms. Tonn	Mr. Etta Tonn
Mr. Verramutch	Mr. Hank U. Verramutch

AT A SQUARE DANCE

Ms. Reel	Mrs. Virginia Reel
Mr. Amandleft	Mr. Al Amandleft
Mr. Toomalou	Mr. Skip Toomalou
Mr. See	Mr. Kurt See

AT A NEW DELHI TAP-DANCE FESTIVAL

Mr. Ingindarain	Mr. Singh Ingindarain

AT A LAS VEGAS CASINO

Ms. Lett	Ms. Rue Lett
Ms. Yourbett	Mrs. Raisa Yourbett
Mr. Getyouten	Mr. Fivel Getyouten
Ms. Sarrloaded	Ms. Di Sarrloaded

Ms. Winner .... Ms. Ima Winner
Ms. LaSevven .... Ms. Ro LaSevven
Mr. Anymorticketsforsigfriedandroy . . .
       Mr. Arthur Anymorticketsforsigfriedandroy
Mr. Zyafivebux .... Mr. Ray Zyafivebux
Mr. Wunmoreroll .... Mr. Jess Wunmoreroll
Mr. Lopoker .... Mr. Hy Lopoker
Mr. Pott .... Mr. Jack Pott
Mr. Ooze .... Mr. Yul Ooze
Ms. Fairinnsquare .... Ms. Yvonne Fairinnsquare
Mr. Yoursleeve .... Mr. Aesop Yoursleeve
Ms. Flush .... Ms. Delta Flush
Mr. Erz .... Mr. Wynn Erz
Mr. Zerz .... Mr. Lou Zerz

AT A NEWSSTAND

Mr. Oddical .... Mr. Perry Oddical
Ms. Zeene .... Ms. Maggie Zeene
Ms. Paper .... Ms. Rita Paper
Mr. Cagotribune .... Mr. Chick Cagotribune

28

Mr. Ittorial .... Mr. Ed Ittorial
Ms. News .... Ms. Dale E. News
Mr. Singform .... Mr. Ray Singform
Ms. Timze .... Ms. Elle A. Timze
Ms. Stigest .... Ms. Rita Stigest
Mr. Loid .... Mr. Tab Loid

AT THE LOUVRE

Mr. Diglianni .... Mr. Moe Diglianni
Ms. Lizzem .... Ms. Rhea Lizzem
Mr. Isstick .... Mr. Art Isstick
Mr. Beele .... Mr. Moe Beele
Mr. Nahlesa .... Mr. Moe Nahleesa
Mr. Errcolor .... Mr. Ward Errcolor
Mr. Ibaster .... Mr. Al Ibaster
Mr. Idbrothercoulddoothat . . .

          Mr. Mike Idbrothercoulddoothat
Mr. Yunbucksforthat .... Mr. Emile Yunbucksforthat
Mr. Esk .... Mr. Ruben Esk

AT JURASSIC PARK

Ms. Assauruss .... Ms. Meg Assauruss

Mr. Ranasorrusrecks .... Mr. Ty Ranasorrusrecks

Ms. Sore .... Ms. Dinah Sore

Ms. Ard .... Ms. Liz Ard

Mr. Zenzadadeep .... Mr. Denny Zenzadadeep

AT THE JIMMY DURANTE MUSEUM

Ms. Dinkadoo .... Ms. Inga Dinkadoo

Mr. Abash .... Mr. Cal Abash

AT A COMEDY CLUB

Mr. Merr .... Mr. Hugh Merr

Mr. King .... Mr. Joe King

Ms. Laff .... Ms. Belle E. Laff

Ms. Ksterr .... Mr. Joe Ksterr

Mr. Rophone .... Mr. Mike Rophone

Ms. Jest .... Ms. Shirley U. Jest

Ms. Frummsirr .... Ms. Vera U. Frummsirr

Mr. Seeriousleefolks .... Mr. Bud Seeriousleefolks

AT A BOOKSTORE

Ms. Flying .... Ms. Vera Flying

Ms. Turner .... Ms. Paige Turner

Mr. Ittyfair .... Mr. Van Ittyfair

Ms. Mainzuvvtheday .... Ms. Rhea Mainzuvvtheday

Mr. Ican .... Mr. Jess Ican

Ms. Jizzuvmadisoncountee Ms. Brie Jizzuvmadisoncountee

Mr. Manpoorman .... Mr. Rich Manpoorman

Ms. Jarr .... Ms. Belle Jarr

Mr. Beedick .... Mr. Moe Beedick

Ms. Ingthere .... Ms. Bea Ingthere

Mr. Lisseeze .... Mr. Yul Lisseeze

Mr. Ellforadonno .... Mr. Abe Ellforadonno

Mr. Misscarroll .... Mr. Chris Misscarroll

Mr. Tayzinferno .... Mr. Don Tayzinferno

Mr. Flewoverthecuckoosnest . . .

Mr. Juan Flewoverthecuckoosnest

Mr. Kantgohomeagain ..... Mr. Hugh Kantgohomeagain

Mr. Izzanisland .... Mr. Norman Izzanisland

AT A GRAMMARIAN'S RETREAT

Ms. Risk .... Ms. Asta Risk

Mr. Acular .... Mr. Vern Acular

Mr. Glingparticiple .... Mr. Dan Glingparticiple

AT A POETRY READING

Ms. Mattapeeya .... Ms. Anna Mattapeeya

Ms. Tinnim .... Ms. Ann Tinnim

Mr. Itterayshun .... Mr. Al Itterayshun

Mr. O'Rick .... Mr. Lem O'Rick

Ms. Poette .... Ms. Ima Poette

Mr. Zeefartsee .... Mr. Art Zeefartsee

AT A COUNTRY CLUB

Mr. Downyournose .... Mr. Luke Downyournose

Ms. Money .... Ms. Lotta Money

Ms. Scriminate .... Ms. Dee Scriminate

Mr. Grate .... Mr. Denny Grate

Ms. Exclusive .... Ms. Zoe Exclusive

Ms. Snobb	Ms. Bea A. Snobb
Ms. Snobb	Ms. Sacha Snobb
Ms. Richest	Ms. Dee Richest
Mr. Neegroze	Mr. Noah Necgroze
Mr. Joozaloud	Mr. Noel Joozaloud
Mr. Estmoonball	Mr. Harv Estmoonball
Mr. Oof	Mr. Al Oof
Mr. Shingskool	Mr. Vinnie Shingskool
Ms. Tont	Ms. Deb U. Tont

3 Paging:

Ms. Immelkingdom . . .
Ms. Ann Immelkingdom

People Likely to Be Paged:

AT A CAT SHOW

Mr. Ishfold	Mr. Scott Ishfold
Ms. Litter	Ms. Kitty Litter
Mr. Icko	Mr. Cal Icko
Mr. Bee	Mr. Tab Bee
Ms. Gora	Ms. Ann Gora
Mr. Ahmeese	Mr. Sy Ahmeese

AT A DOG SHOW

Ms. Merreyener .... Ms. Vy Merreyener

Mr. Erd .... Mr. Shep Erd

Mr. Beeryanhuskee .... Mr. Sy Beeryanhuskee

Ms. Itthound .... Ms. Bess Itthound

Mr. Zund .... Mr. "Doc" Zund

Ms. Gull .... Ms. Bea Gull

Ms. Aturecollie .... Ms. Minnie Aturecollie

Mr. Dardpoodle .... Mr. Stan Dardpoodle

AT THE ZOO

Mr. Aff .... Mr. Jer Aff

Ms. Konda .... Ms. Anna Konda

Mr. Eena .... Mr. Hy Eena

Mr. Essmonkee .... Mr. Reese Essmonkee

Ms. O'Monkeeze .... Ms. Beryl O'Monkeeze

Mr. Nahceruss .... Mr. Ray Nahceruss

Mr. Ifferous .... Mr. Herb Ifferous

IN A PET STORE

Mr. Ster .... Mr. Ham Ster
Mr. Bill .... Mr. Jer Bill

AT THE AQUARIUM

Mr. Merhead .... Mr. Ham Merhead
Mr. Cuda .... Mr. Barry Cuda
Ms. Troute .... Ms. Brooke Troute
Mr. Eel .... Mr. Maurie Eel
Ms. Ecktrickeel .... Ms. Elle Ecktrickeel
Ms. Coshark .... Ms. May Coshark
Mr. Tee .... Mr. Manny Tee

4 Matt Chemmupp

*Connect the Given Name on the Left to the
Surname on the Right:*

1. Hans		A.	Wayseed
2. Ray		B.	Umm
3. Meg		C.	Kobabble
4. Hugh		D.	Mentuvsylense
5. Sy		E.	Enbudda
6. Ken		F	Ishun
7. Kal C.		G.	Enfeet
8. Moe		H.	Nonmyparade
9. Madge		I.	Weetalk
10. Cara		J.	Alomaynea
11. Belle E.		K.	Button
12. Brett		L.	Saidamouthful

ANSWERS:

1G 2H 3J 4L 5C 6I 7B 8D 9F 10A 11K 12E

37

5 Paging:

Mr. Norshine . . .

Mr. Ray Norshine

People Likely to Be Paged:

ON THE WEATHER CHANNEL

Mr. Dwave	Mr. Cole Dwave
Mr. Uvsnow	Mr. Dustin Uvsnow
Mr. Presher	Mr. Hy Presher
Mr. Uvsunshine	Mr. Ray Uvsunshine
Mr. Daze	Mr. Sonny Daze
Mr. Needaze	Mr. Ray Needaze
Mr. Foon	Mr. Ty Foon

Mr. Cane .... Mr. Harry Cane
Mr. Tide .... Mr. Hy Tide
Mr. Klone .... Mr. Sy Klone
Ms. Buttkool .... Ms. Sunny Buttkool
Ms. Reclipse .... Ms. Luna Reclipse
Ms. Showers .... Ms. April Showers
Mr. Eeklipse .... Mr. Saul R. Eeklipse
Mr. Front .... Mr. Cole Front
Ms. Mommetter .... Ms. Anna Mommetter
Mr. Elleekwinocks .... Mr. Vern Elleekwinocks
Mr. Ickfront .... Mr. Art Ickfront
Mr. Dwop .... Mr. Dwane Dwop
Mr. Midd .... Mr. Hugh Midd
Mr. Sheer .... Mr. Wynn Sheer
Chief Owingclouds .... Chief Bill Owingclouds
Mr. Stiss .... Mr. Sol Stiss
Dr. Ooshun .... Dr. Paul Ooshun

6 Paging:
Mr. Eukayshun . . .
Mr. Ed Eukayshun

People Likely to Be Paged:

IN THE FACULTY LOUNGE

Ms. Students .... Ms. Deena Students

Mr. Strarr .... Mr. Reggie Strarr

Dr. Ossofee .... Dr. Phil Ossofee

Mr. Historee .... Mr. Art Historee

Dr. Otticks .... Dr. Sammy Otticks

Dr. Thropolojee .... Dr. Ann Thropolojee

Dr. Sigh .... Dr. Polly Sigh

Dr. Jebra .... Dr. Al Jebra
Dr. Kewluss .... Dr. Kal Kewluss
Dr. Molojee .... Dr. Eddy Molojee
Dr. Manittees .... Dr. Hugh Manittees
Dr. Kuptest .... Dr. Mae Kuptest
Dr. Intist .... Dr. Sy Intist
Dr. Urreducation .... Dr. Hy Urreducation
Dr. Atomy .... Dr. Ann Atomy
Dr. Kwunohwun .... Dr. Sy Kwunohwun
Dr. Niversity .... Dr. Hugh Niversity
Dr. Klass .... Dr. Jim Klass

IN A DORMITORY

Mr. Klasses .... Mr. "Skip" Klasses
Mr. Lobb .... Mr. "Ace" Lobb
Ms. Ingcloze .... Ms. Cher Ingcloze
Mr. Dreeroom .... Mr. Lon Dreeroom
Mr. Riculate .... Mr. Matt Riculate
Ms. Leeger .... Ms. Ivy Leeger

Ms. Mate .... Ms. Rue Mate
Mr. Eckkallhome .... Mr. Cole Eckkallhome
Ms. Date .... Ms. Anita Date
Mr. Deeuss .... Mr. Stu Deeuss
Mr. Less .... Mr. Whit Less
Mr. Dent .... Mr. Stu Dent

AT THE LIBRARY

Mr. Shunary .... Mr. Dick Shunary
Mr. Decimal .... Mr. Dewey Decimal
Mr. Sauruss .... Mr. Theo Sauruss
Mr. Rophilm .... Mr. Mike Rophilm
Mr. Books .... Mr. Tex Books
Ms. Sirch .... Ms. Rhea Sirch
Mr. Fabetticalorder .... Mr. Al Fabetticalorder
Ms. Kwiette .... Ms. Bea Kwiette
Mr. Talking .... Mr. Noah Talking
Mr. Gurlz .... Mr. Meade Gurlz
Mr. Guyze .... Mr. Meade Guyze

IN ART CLASS

Ms. Errperspective .... Ms. Lynn E. Errperspective

Mr. Supplize .... Mr. Art Supplize

Ms. Perspective .... Ms. Ariel Perspective

Mr. Iggraffee .... Mr. Cal Iggraffee

Mr. Model .... Mr. Newt Model

Mr. Luvfroote .... Mr. Beau Luvfroote

IN A SCIENCE CLASS

Ms. Tube .... Ms. Tess Tube

Ms. O'Second .... Ms. Nan O'Second

Ms. Ment .... Ms. Ellie Ment

Mr. Tiffickmethud .... Mr. Sy N. Tiffickmethud

Mr. Ment .... Mr. X. Perry Ment

Ms. Seckshun .... Ms. Di Seckshun

Ms. Kerr .... Ms. Bea Kerr

Ms. Icks .... Ms. Jeanette Icks

Ms. Splysing .... Ms. Jean Splysing

Mr. Sunnburner .... Mr. Ben Sunnburner

Ms. Keeway .... Ms. Millie Keeway

IN ELEMENTARY SCHOOL

Ms. Andcheralike	Ms. Cher Andcheralike
Mr. Ess	Mr. Reese Ess
Ms. Hayveyourself	Ms. Bea Hayveyourself
Ms. Shunn	Ms. Ella Q. Shunn
Mr. Unplann	Mr. Les Unplann
Ms. Tenshun	Ms. Dee Tenshun
Mr. Sleef	Mr. Lew Sleef

AT A GRADUATION CEREMONY

Ms. Gree	Ms. Dee Gree
Ms. Motter	Ms. Alma Motter
Ms. Ay	Ms. Bea Ay

7 Paging:

Ms. Ailia . . . Ms. Janet Ailia

People Likely to Be Paged:

AT THE MASTERS AND JOHNSON INSTITUTE

Mr. Off	Mr. Jack Off
Ms. Trayshun	Ms. Cass Trayshun
Ms. Tickle	Ms. Tess Tickle
Ms. Frodite	Ms. Irma Frodite
Mr. Aysheeyo	Mr. Phil Aysheeyo
Mr. Jobb	Mr. Hans Jobb
Ms. Brator	Ms. Vi Brator
Ms. Whyjelly	Ms. Kay Whyjelly

Ms. Efframm .... Ms. Di Efframm

Mr. Teruss .... Mr. Hugh Teruss

Ms. Ache .... Ms. Hedda Ache

Ms. Thingoze .... Ms. Annie Thingoze

Mr. Promiscuous .... Mr. Hy Lee Promiscuous

Ms. Sillin .... Ms. Penny Sillin

Ms. Gentle .... Ms. Bea Gentle

Mr. Meupp .... Mr. Ty Meupp

Mr. Ulate .... Mr. E. Jack Ulate

AT THE NEW DELHI BRANCH OF
MASTERS AND JOHNSON

Ms. Offmee .... Ms. Gita Offmee

Ms. Meoff .... Ms. Gita Meoff

AT THE ACAPULCO BRANCH OF
MASTERS AND JOHNSON

Senorita Deekurtz .... Senorita Maya Deekurtz

**BOOKS AVAILABLE AT THE
MASTERS AND JOHNSON LIBRARY**

Get to Know Your Dog, by Bea Stiality
It Ain't the Size That Counts,
by Millie Meter

AT AN ORGY IN THE CATSKILLS

Mr. Twah .... Mr. Menashe Twah

AT A SINGLES BAR

Mr. Howaya .... Mr. Hy Howaya

Ms. Noyoo .... Ms. Dona Noyoo

Mr. Smeebuthaventwemetbefor . . .

　　　　　　Mr. X. Hugh Smeebuthaventwemetbefor

Ms. Aroundhere .... Ms. Liv Aroundhere

Mr. Membayoo .... Mr. Ira Membayoo

Mr. Attractive .... Mr. Meyer Attractive

Mr. Thisseattaken .... Mr. Iz Thisseattaken

Mr. Byooadrink .... Mr. Ken I. Byooadrink

Mr. Beimeiself .... Mr. Chaim Beimeiself

Ms. Foryurthawts .... Ms. Penny Foryurthawts

Mr. Atthoselegs .... Mr. Luke Atthoselegs

Mr. Antbeeleevthatbut ..... Mr. Ike Antbeeleevthatbut

Ms. Howhewooldbeeinbed Mr. Wanda
                        Howhewooldbeeinbed

Mr. Drink .... Mr. Juan A. Drink

Ms. Danz .... Ms. Tawana Danz

Mr. Uliketokizmee .... Mr. Howard Uliketokizmee

Ms. Dacradle .... Ms. Robin Dacradle

Ms. Okie .... Ms. Carrie Okie

Mr. Havyurnumber .... Mr. Ken I. Havyurnumber

Mr. Onthepill .... Mr. R. Hugh Onthepill

Mr. Phuk .... Mr. Juan A. Phuk

Ms. Placeoryurs .... Mrs. Maya Placeoryurs

8 Paging:

Mr. Galeegull . . .
Mr. Lee Galeegull

People Likely to Be Paged:

AT THE POLICEMAN'S BALL

Mr. Automatic	Mr. Sammy Automatic
Mr. Club	Mr. Billy Club
Mr. Rollcar	Mr. Pat Rollcar
Mr. Twelve	Mr. Adam Twelve
Ms. Orrder	Ms. Lauren Orrder
Ms. Koyoperayshun	Ms. Dee Koyoperayshun
Mr. Menn	Mr. Orestes Menn

Mr. Yurwrites .... Mr. Reed Yurwrites
Mr. Danno .... Mr. Booker Danno

IN A COURT OF LAW

Ms. Wrights .... Ms. Sybil Wrights
Ms. Suit .... Ms. Sybil Suit
Ms. Liberteeze .... Ms. Sybil Liberteeze
Ms. Yurritehand .... Ms. Raisa Yurritehand
Ms. Shill .... Ms. Judy Shill
Mr. Mobb .... Mr. Lynch Mobb
Mr. Ickate .... Mr. Jude Ickate
Mr. O'Wrights .... Mr. Bill O'Wrights
Mr. Ness .... Mr. Whit Ness
Mr. Oozhjunne .... Mr. Cole Oozhjunne
Mr. Ofhabeascorpus .... Mr. Whit Ofhabeascorpus
Mr. Pole .... Mr. Lou Pole
Mr. Tee .... Mr. Gil Tee
Ms. Mycase .... Ms. Iris Mycase
Ms. Sclosed .... Ms. Kay Sclosed

IN PRISON

Mr. Cyde	Mr. Homer Cyde
Mr. Erree	Mr. Rob Erree
Mr. Up	Mr. Hans Up
Mr. Killya	Mr. Oral Killya
Ms. Enabette	Ms. Ada Enabette
Mr. Content	Mr. Mal Content
Ms. Bezlemint	Ms. Em Bezlemint
Mr. Dasystem	Mr. Buck Dasystem
Mr. Inkwent	Mr. Del Inkwent

WANTED BY INTERPOL

*Reward for Any Information Leading
to the Arrest of the Following Criminals:*

From **ZIMBABWE:**
   Moe Swanted

From **FRANCE:**
   Jacques Guse

From **TRANSYLVANIA:**
   Count Affitter

From **FRANCE:**
   John Darm

From **ITALY:**
   Carrie Benarrie

From **VIETNAM:**
   Ho Dupp

From **SWEDEN:**
   Lars Ceny

From **ITALY:**
   "Ma" Feeya

From **GERMANY:**
   Hans Up

From **JAPAN:**
   Fugi Tive

9 On a First-Name Basis

or

Ah, Sweet Miss Terry of Life

In the **STELLA** the night, I **WANDA** around the house looking for **MIKIE** to my **OTTO**. It's like playing Hide and **ZEKE** with them. Everywhere I think they might **BEA**, they aren't. **WHITNEY** pads on, I **NEIL** on the floor and **LUKE** under the couch. **ARTHUR** keys there? Nope! I **EMMA** wreck. It's so **STEPHY** in here, and, of course, the air conditioner is on the **FRITZ**. Sweat begins to **FLO** from my pores. Feeling a bit woozy, I stand up and **ILENE** on the table, and there are my keys!

My mother appears and asks, "**JAMAL** the letter I gave you yesterday?"

"Yes," I reply. "**IMELDA** letter."

She comes over to me **HOLDEN** up a copy of *WARREN Peace*. "**EVERETT** this?" she asks.

There oughta be a **LAURA** something against people asking so many questions so early in the morning. I shake my head. "No."

"**ALFRED** it and liked it a lot. **TAWANA** borrow it? It wouldn't hurt **HUGH** to **RITA** book every now and then."

Again, I shake my head. "No." I let out a **SY. SVEN WILMA** learn not to bother me when I'm in a hurry?

Once outside, I quickly **MARGE** over to the green **CHEVY**, of which I am now the proud **ONA**. I had **ELISE**, but now I own it **SCOTT** free, having paid it off in **JUNE. TRU**, it's not a **PORTIA**, but as long as I'm not **OWEN** any money on it, it's good enough.

I notice a **PENNEY** on the floor **MATT**. I know it won't make me **RICH**, but I pick it up and put it in my pocket **JUSTIN** case. **HUGH NEVILLE** know **SVEN EWELL BEA** short just one **PENNEY**. And, **LEM** me **TALIA, ANITA** good-luck charm these days.

Not wanting to **BUCK** the traffic on the highway, I drive through the **GLENN**.

OLIVER sudden **ANN** animal runs in front of my car. It is neither a wolf **NORA** coyote. Whatever it is, I spot him **JUSTIN** the **NICK** of time and swerve, running over some **ROXANNE** bottles. I **HERA** crunch. It's a flat tire. I **FREIDA JACK** from its well and **CHAIM** just about to try to **LUCINDA** lug nuts **SVEN** a motorist drives by.

ZOE says, "**EWELL** need my help, **JESS?**"

"I don't believe that a woman should do **MANUEL** labor. If we were in a boat, I **WOODROW**," he says **OZZIE** changes the tire and then wipes his **HANS** on a rag.

54

OZZIE heads back to his car, I thank him in **EARNEST** for being **DENISE** man **THAD** he is.

"**EUNICE** too," he says. "**ISRAEL** pleasure to help **HUGH.**"

I watch him drive off and **ASAI** put my hand in my pocket to get **MIKIE** I feel the **PENNEY** and smile. It's **SHIRLEY BEN MAI LUCKY** day.

THEA END

(**TOBY** Continued)

10 Paging:

Mr. Ingroom . . .
Mr. Wade Ingroom

People Likely to Be Paged:

AT THE PHARMACY

Ms. O'Cyn .... Ms. Ann O'Cyn

Mr. Kahseltzer .... Mr. Al Kahseltzer

Ms. Uretic .... Ms. Di Uretic

Mr. Lenall .... Mr. Ty Lenall

Mr. Izer .... Mr. Adam Izer

Ms. Bitussin .... Ms. Roe Bitussin

AT THE HOSPITAL WAITING ROOM

Dr. Zeeziz	Dr. Dee Zeeziz
Mr. Ookawfull	Mr. Yul Ookawfull
Mr. Fever	Mr. Hy Fever
Nurse Terr	Nurse Cathy Terr
Mr. Aitillherneeya	Mr. Hy Aitillherneeya
Mr. O'Scope	Mr. Arthur O'Scope
Mr. Ummenema	Mr. Barry Ummenema
Ms. Arrear	Ms. Di Arrear
Ms. Pingwound	Ms. Gay Pingwound
Nurse Chur	Nurse Sue Chur
Ms. Dripp	Ms. Ivy Dripp
Ms. Pressed	Ms. Dee Pressed
Mr. Attack	Mr. Art Attack
Ms. Jina	Ms. Ann Jina
Mr. Nisitus	Mr. Sy Nisitus
Ms. Neemic	Ms. Ann Neemic
Mr. Etts	Mr. Rick Etts
Mr. Pocondriack	Mr. Hy Pocondriack
Mr. Outforms	Mr. Phil Outforms

AT THE DERMATOLOGIST'S OFFICE

Mr. Byno	Mr. Al Byno
Mr. Skins	Mr. "Redd" Skins
Dr. Ollojee	Dr. Dermot Ollojee
Dr. Thatboil	Dr. Lance Thatboil
Mr. O'Mineloshun	Mr. Cal O'Mineloshun
Dr. Upyourface	Dr. Claire Upyourface

AT AN ITALIAN DERMATOLOGIST'S OFFICE

Ms. Zitts	Ms. Maura Zitts

AT THE PODIATRIST'S OFFICE

Dr. Support	Dr. Arch Support
Dr. Uss	Dr. Cal Uss
Dr. Peedickshooz	Dr. Arthur Peedickshooz

AT THE PROCTOLOGIST'S OFFICE

Mr. Antsiddown	Mr. Ike Antsiddown
Ms. Bagg	Ms. N. Emma Bagg

Dr. Oscopy .... Dr. Colin Oscopy
Ms. Hynde .... Ms. Bea Hynde
Dr. Oxx .... Dr. Budd Oxx

AT THE GOLF COURSE

Dr. Dooin .... Dr. Howie Dooin
Dr. Havalook .... Dr. Les Havalook
Dr. Woolsample .... Dr. Stu Woolsample
Dr. Esstheeziologist .... Dr. Ann Esstheeziologist
Dr. Scopic .... Dr. Arthur Scopic
Dr. Atricks .... Dr. Petey Atricks
Dr. Kyatrist .... Dr. Sy Kyatrist
Dr. Kologist .... Dr. Sy Kologist
Dr. Bloodpreshir .... Dr. Hy Bloodpreshir
Dr. Tykoagulant .... Dr. Ann Tykoagulant
Dr. Ernityward .... Dr. Matt Ernityward
Dr. Keyotomee .... Dr. Trey Keyotomee
Dr. Thermometer .... Dr. Oral Thermometer
Dr. Erry .... Dr. Serge Erry

Dr. O'Gram	....	Dr. Angie O'Gram
Dr. Ductible	....	Dr. Dee Ductible
Dr. Practice	....	Dr. Mal Practice

AT THE DENTIST'S OFFICE

Dr. Itosis	....	Dr. Hal Itosis
Mr. Lahr	....	Mr. Moe Lahr
Dr. Kaye	....	Dr. Dee Kaye
Dr. Ling	....	Dr. Phil Ling
Dr. Ennist	....	Dr. Hy G. Ennist
Dr. Caine	....	Dr. Nova Caine
Ms. Vitus	....	Ms. Ginger Vitus
Ms. Dayshun	....	Ms. Flora Dayshun
Ms. Ninetooth	....	Ms. Kay Ninetooth
Mr. Datooth	....	Mr. Chip Datooth
Mr. Backenrelax	....	Mr. Sid Backenrelax
Dr. Dontist	....	Dr. Perry O. Dontist

AT THE BETTY FORD CLINIC

Mr. Stopp .... Mr. Kent Stopp

Ms. Fettamin .... Ms. Ann Fettamin

Ms. Tivz .... Ms. Sadie Tivz

Ms. Itchuitz .... Ms. Barb Itchuitz

Mr. Killers .... Mr. Payne Killers

Ms. Eeyum .... Ms. Val Eeyum

Ms. Wynn .... Ms. Hera Wynn

Mr. Umden .... Mr. Opie Umden

Mr. Zerr .... Mr. Abe Hugh Zerr

Mr. Podermickneedle ...... My Hy Podermickneedle

Ms. Naline .... Ms. Mae Naline

Ms. Ingneedles .... Ms. Cher Ingneedles

Ms. Nyal .... Ms. Dee Nyal

Nurse Nanalysis .... Nurse Uri Nanalysis

Dr. Toxx .... Dr. Dee Toxx

Mr. Drawal .... Mr. Whit Drawal

Ms. Covery .... Mrs. Rhea Covery

Ms. O'Rexic .... Mrs. Ann O'Rexic

Mr. Leemic .... Mr. "Bull" Leemic

Mr. Coholism .... Mr. Al Coholism

Ms. Teeze .... Ms. Dee Teeze

Ms. Drink .... Ms. Anita Drink

Ms. Isliztaloralwaysthere ... Ms. Vi Isliztaloralwaysthere

AT THE ACAPULCO BRANCH OF THE
BETTY FORD CLINIC

Senor Dust .... Senor Angel Dust

Senor Lastdrink .... Senor Juan Lastdrink

Roommates at a Retirement Home

- Al Tacocker, Rick Eddyleggs, & Hardy Hearing
- Di Per & Kay O'Pectate
- Gerry Attrick & Lon Jevittee
- Leigh Verspot & Vera Gosveins
- Ben Tover & Shaquille Dover
- Hugh Felldown, Kent Gettup, & Ken U. Helpmeeup
- Arthur Ittick & Kent Walkanymore
- Al Tzimer & Drew Ablank
- Hugh Doanlooksogood & Izzie Deadyet

11 Paging:

Mr. Openspaces . . .
Mr. Wyatt Openspaces

People Likely to Be Paged:

IN THE OLD WEST

Mr. Lerr	Mr. Russ Lerr
Mr. Ellupsumgrubb	Mr. Russ Elupsumgrubb
Ms. Deeoh	Ms. Roe Deeoh
Mr. Wagon	Mr. Chuck Wagon
Mr. Hawk	Mr. Tom A. Hawk
Mr. Tom	Mr. Tom Tom

Mr. Ahroo .... Mr. Buck Ahroo
Mr. Itt .... Mr. Larry Itt
Mr. Uffpardner .... Mr. Shawn Uffpardner
Ms. Horse .... Ms. Rhoda Horse
Ms. Noelcowhand .... Ms. Ima Noelcowhand
Mr. Oon .... Mr. Sal Oon
Mr. Errdhanz .... Mr. Hy Errdhanz
Mr. Noon .... Mr. Hy Noon
Mr. Awatha .... Mr. Hy Awatha
Ms. Iff .... Ms. Cher Iff
Mr. Ranger .... Mr. Lon Ranger
Ms. O'Sabee .... Ms. Kim O'Sabee
Mr. Antee .... Mr. Virgil Antee
Mr. Ingbull .... Mr. Sid Ingbull
Mr. Onammo .... Mr. Jer Onammo
Mr. Terzlasstand .... Mr. Gus Terzlasstand

AT A RODEO IN INDIA

Ms. Longlittledoggie .... Ms. Gita Longlittledoggie

AT A RODEO IN BEIJING

Mr. Hatt .... Mr. Kow Boi Hatt

ON A FARM

Mr. Est .... Mr. Harv Est

Ms. Perr .... Ms. Rhea Perr

Mr. Lowe .... Mr. Sy Lowe

Mr. Goat .... Mr. Billy Goat

Ms. Eegoat .... Ms. Nan Eegoat

Ms. Cropper .... Ms. Cher Cropper

Ms. Weeee .... Ms. Sue Weeee

Mr. Enns .... Mr. Chick Enns

Mr. Ennfeed .... Mr. Chick Ennfeed

Mr. Ennkoop .... Mr. Chick Ennkoop

Ms. Zeetoats .... Ms. Mare Zeetoats

Ms. Lambzeetyvee .... Ms. Lil Lambzeetyvee

Mr. Kropps .... Mr. Dustin Kropps

Ms. Deetee .... Ms. Dee Deetee

Ms. Oohre .... Ms. Min Oohre

Mr. Lizer .... Mr. Ferdi Lizer

ON A RUSSIAN FARM

Ms. Barn .... Ms. Raisa Barn

ON A SWEDISH FARM

Mr. Spost .... Mr. Sven Spost

IN OUTER SPACE

Ms. Exxy .... Ms. Gail Exxy

Ms. Roid .... Ms. Esther Roid

Ms. Longwayfromhome .... Ms. Vera Longwayfromhome

Ms. Meupscottie .... Ms. Bea Meupscottie

Ms. Inn .... Ms. Ailie Inn

Mr. Nermodule .... Mr. Lou Nermodule

Ms. Roarbit .... Ms. Luna Roarbit

Mr. Nereclipse .... Ms. Lou Nereclipse

Mr. Ettship .... Mr. Rock Ettship

Mr. Effo .... Mr. Hugh Effo

12 Paging:

King Altee . . . King Roy Altee

Kings Likely to Be Paged:

- THE KING WHO'S HARD TO GET TO: **Moe Taroundthecastle**
- THE REALLY STUPID KING: **King Dumb**
- THE KING WHO'S A BIG ROGER MILLER FAN:
  King Uvtheroad
- THE KING WHO LIKES REALLY PHYSICAL CHILDREN'S
  GAMES: **King Uvthehill**
- THE FLATULENT RUSSIAN KING: **Czar E. I. Pharted**

Knights Likely to Be Paged:

- THE JEWISH KNIGHT: **Sir Cumscision**
- THE SNEAKY KNIGHT: **Sir Uptishuss**
- THE KNIGHT WHO PREVENTS ELECTRICAL FIRES:
  Sir Cutbreaker
- THE DISCREET KNIGHT: **Sir Cumspect**
- THE DRUNKEN KNIGHT: **Sir Osis**
- THE WOODWORKING KNIGHT: **Sir Cularsaw**
- THE KNIGHT WHO TAKES A LONG TIME GETTING THERE:
  Sir Cuitous
- THE KNIGHT WITH LOTS OF SHARP TEETH: **Sir Ated**
- THE AUTO-MECHANIC KNIGHT: **Sir Visstation**
- THE TALL SQUIGGLY KNIGHT: **Sir Pentine**
- THE KNIGHT WHO RESEMBLES SALVADOR DALI:
  Sir Realist
- THE SOUTHERN CALIFORNIA KNIGHT: **Sir Fsallday**
- THE KNIGHT NOBODY NEEDS: **Sir Pluss**
- THE KNIGHT WITH A RED NOSE: **Sir Cusclown**

- THE KNIGHT WHO'S DONE BETTER THAN ANYONE EXPECTED: **Sir Passedallexpectations**
- THE DARWINIAN KNIGHT: **Sir Vivaluvthefittest**
- THE KNIGHT WHO SPIES ON PEOPLE: **Sir Veilance**
- THE GLAZED KNIGHT: **Sir Ammick**
- THE KNIGHT WHO'S GREAT TO LISTEN TO: **Sir Roundsound**
- THE KNIGHT WHO'S ALWAYS DOING THE UNEXPECTED: **Sir Prizedyoudidenteye**
- THE CHEERFUL KNIGHT: **Sir Tenleyizzanicedayizzentit**
- THE BLISSFUL KNIGHT: **Sir Reen**
- THE KNIGHTS WHO TAKES POLLS: **Sir Vey**
- THE COMMANDO KNIGHT: **Sir Chandistroy**
- THE FEMALE KNIGHT: **Sir Vix**
- THE BEEFY KNIGHT: **Sir Loin**
- THE STAND-IN KNIGHT: **Sir Ragett**
- THE SHALLOW KNIGHT: **Sir Fyss**
- THE ANGRY KNIGHT: **Sir Lee**
- THE KNIGHT WHO OVERCAME OBSTACLES: **Sir Mount**

- THE INSANE KNIGHT: **Sir Tifyable**
- THE FORMER YUGOSLAVIAN KNIGHT: **Sir Beaucroayshun**

Ladies Di Likely to Be Paged:

Most people don't know it, but Lady Diana was but one of many candidates on a long list from which Prince Charles chose his bride. If he had chosen differently, the royal family might have been able to page the Lady Di who:

- IS A BLOND BOMBSHELL: **Lady Di Mondsarragirlsbestfriend**
- HAD BAD STOMACH TROUBLE: **Lady Di Verticulitis**
- IS NO LONGER WITH US: **Lady Di Dandwentooheaven**
- IS A GREAT JOKE TELLER: **Lady Di Tellyoudawunabout**
- IS VERY EXPLOSIVE: **Lady Di Nomite**
- DOESN'T WANT TO GET PREGNANT: **Lady Di Aphram**
- IS VERY PREACHY: **Lady Di Dacktick**
- IS A WITCH: **Lady Di Abolical**
- YOU CAN SEE THROUGH: **Lady Di Aphenous**

- IS REALLY ORDINARY: **Lady Di Madozen**
- IS A REAL NIGHT PERSON: **Lady Di Nandance**
- IS A REAL LOOSE WOMAN: **Lady Di Madance**
- HAS A SHORT ATTENTION SPAN: **Lady Di Gress**
- IS INCONTINENT: **Lady Di Per**
- IS ALWAYS ARGUING: **Lady Di Atribe**
- IS TOO FAT: **Lady Di Ette**
- WITH A BAD HEART: **Lady Di Lantin**

13 Paging:

Ms. Ooteeful . . .
Ms. Bea Ooteeful

People Likely to Be Paged:

AT THE GYM

Mr. Mongus	Mr. Hugh Mongus
Ms. Fupp	Ms. Bea Fupp
Ms. Ells	Ms. Barb Ells
Mr. Ories	Mr. Cal Ories
Mr. Uss	Mr. Cal Uss
Mr. Toids	Mr. Del Toids
Mr. Strings	Mr. Ham Strings
Mr. Impact	Mr. Hy Impact

Ms. Ziztence .... Ms. Rhea Ziztence
Ms. Wingmasheen .... Ms. Roe Wingmasheen
Ms. Dorphins .... Ms. Ann Dorphins
Mr. Builder .... Mr. Buddy Builder
Ms. Kamussel .... Ms. Mae Kamussel
Mr. Doothis .... Mr. Ken U. Doothis
Mr. Horse .... Mr. Charlie Horse
Ms. Amint .... Ms. Lynn Amint
Ms. O'Tard .... Ms. Leigh O'Tard
Mr. Beat .... Mr. Chaim Beat
Mr. Bushed .... Mr. Chaim Bushed

IN A BARBER SHOP

Ms. Urpole .... Ms. Barb Urpole
Ms. Urchare .... Ms. Barb Urchare
Mr. Ittleoffthesides .... Mr. Al Ittleoffthesides
Mr. Ittleoffthetop .... Mr. Al Ittleoffthetop
Mr. Zorr .... Mr. Ray Zorr
Mr. Zorrstrap .... Mr. Ray Zorrstrap

IN A BEAUTY PARLOR

Ms. Ooteeparlor .... Ms. Bea Ooteeparlor
Mr. Olin .... Mr. Lan Olin
Mr. Uvolay .... Mr. Earl Uvolay
Ms. Shill .... Ms. Fay Shill
Ms. Cure .... Ms. Patty Cure
Ms. Pinn .... Ms. Bobby Pinn
Ms. Job .... Ms. Di Job
Ms. Haircut .... Ms. Anita Haircut
Ms. Hive .... Ms. Bea Hive
Ms. Boy .... Ms. Paige Boy

AT A FASHION SHOW

Mrs. Skirt .... Mrs. Minnie Skirt
Mr. Kinn .... Mr. Manny Kinn
Mr. Fashion .... Mr. Hy Fashion
Mr. Chest .... Mr. Noah Chest
Mr. Heels .... Mr. Hy Heels
Ms. Maid .... Ms. Taylor Maid

Mr. Onn .... Mr. Ray Onn

Ms. Lining .... Ms. Felice Lining

Mr. Down .... Mr. Mark Down

Mr. Terrayshuns .... Mr. Al Terrayshuns

Mr. Fein .... Mr. Fitz Fein

Mr. Anngedditforyawholesale . . .

                        Mr. Ike Anngedditforyawholesale

Mr. Tye .... Mr. Beau Tye

14 Hugh Decide

A MULTIPLE-CHOICE QUIZ

Luke Upthere .... Astronomer or Proctologist

Hy Azakite .... Baloonist or Drug Czar

Schlomo Shin .... Octogenarian or Israeli
Special Effects Whiz

Albie Seeinya .... Womanizer or Bungee Jumper

Yetta Nother .... Nymphomaniac or Statistician

Buck L. Upp .... Flight Attendant or Dominatrix

Sal Oote .... Italian Army Officer or Wine
Taster

Sal Ooshun .... Master Detective or Chemist

Zack O. Shitt .... Garbage Collector or Politician

Henny Bodyhome .... Burglar or Jehovah's Witness

Lil Dipper .... Candy Maker or Midget Porn
Star

Lou Sazagooz .... Valium Addict or Contortionist

15 Paging:

Mr. Strapp . . .

Mr. Jacques Strapp

People Likely to Be Paged:

AT A BASEBALL GAME

Mr. N'Delay .... Mr. Ray N'Delay

Ms. Nuts .... Ms. Pia Nuts

Mr. Out .... Mr. Doug Out

Mr. Chwarmer .... Mr. Ben Chwarmer

Mr. Unn .... Mr. Homer Unn

Mr. Safe .... Mr. Hugh R. Safe

Mr. Slam .... Mr. Grant Slam
Mr. Penn .... Mr. "Bull" Penn
Mr. Beerhere .... Mr. Cole Beerhere
Ms. Liefpitcher .... Ms. Rhea Liefpitcher
Ms. Innbagg .... Ms. Roz Innbagg
Mr. Issleegher .... Mr. Tex Issleegher
Mr. Ondeck .... Mr. Izzy Ondeck
Mr. Andinside .... Mr. Hy Andinside
Mr. Fly .... Mr. "Pop" Fly
Mr. Outt .... Mr. Hugh R. Outt

AT A FOOTBALL GAME

Ms. Perbowl .... Ms. Sue Perbowl
Ms. Bohl .... Ms. Rose Bohl
Ms. Torbowl .... Ms. Gay Torbowl
Mr. Defense .... Mr. Nick L. Defense
Mr. Penalty .... Mr. Holden Penalty
Ms. Play .... Ms. Rhea Play
Mr. Fishalturff .... Mr. Artie Fishalturff

Mr. Stringpull	....	Mr. Ham Stringpull
Mr. Delines	....	Mr. Sy Delines
Mr. Tend	....	Mr. Ty Tend
Mr. Daball	....	Mr. Spike Daball
Mr. Nalfoul	....	Mr. Percy Nalfoul
Mr. Mout	....	Mr. Ty Mout
Mr. Wonfordagipper	....	Mr. Wynn Wonfordagipper

AT A HOCKEY GAME

Ms. Soff	....	Ms. Faye Soff
Mr. O'Shay	....	Mr. Rick O'Shay
Ms. Smask	....	Ms. Faye Smask
Mr. Boney	....	Mr. Sam Boney

AT A BOWLING ALLEY

Mr. Ling	....	Mr. Bo Ling
Mr. Lingpin	....	Mr. Bo Lingpin
Mr. Lingball	....	Mr. Bo Lingball
Mr. Lingshoes	....	Mr. Bo Lingshoes

Mr. Lingalley .... Mr. Bo Longalley
Mr. Mattickpinsetter .... Mr. Otto Mattickpinsetter

AT A BASKETBALL GAME

Mr. Assonsquaregarden .... Mr. Matt Assonsquaregarden
Ms. Seeddubbelay .... Ms. Ann Seeddubbelay
Mr. Bounds .... Mr. Otto Bounds
Ms. Bound .... Ms. Rhea Bound
Ms. Bock .... Ms. Rhea Bock
Mr. Daball .... Mr. Duncan Daball
Mr. Uvdarimm .... Mr. Abe Uvdarimm
Mr. Five .... Mr. Hy Five

AT A BOXING MATCH

Mr. Inganweaving .... Mr. Bob Inganweaving
Ms. Lowthebelt .... Ms. Bea Lowthebelt
Mr. Oh .... Mr. T. K. Oh

AT A TENNIS MATCH

Mr. Anywan	Mr. Dennis Anywan
Mr. Cort	Mr. Clay Cort
Mr. Dimagain	Mr. "Ace" Dimagain

AT THE OLYMPICS

Mr. Sledd	Mr. Bob Sledd
Mr. Jumpp	Mr. Hy Jumpp
Mr. Diver	Mr. Hy Diver
Mr. Vault	Mr. Paul Vault
Ms. Lifft	Ms. Cher Lifft
Ms. Kathlon	Ms. Dee Kathlon
Ms. Thonn	Mr. Mara Thonn
Ms. Spinn	Ms. Cyd Spinn
Mr. Hurdles	Mr. Hy Hurdles
Mr. Churee	Mr. Art Churee
Mr. Nasticks	Mr. Jim Nasticks
Ms. Medal	Ms. Golda Medal

AT A SKY DIVING EVENT
Mr. Tittude .... Mr. Al Tittude

AT A SKEET SHOOT
Mr. Pihjin .... Mr. Clay Pihjin

AT THE INDIANAPOLIS 500
Ms. Carrera .... Ms. Portia Carrera
Ms. Darado .... Ms. Elle Darado
Mr. Baker .... Mr. Stu D. Baker
Ms. Ville .... Ms. Bonnie Ville
Ms. Vett .... Ms. Cora Vett
Ms. Baroo .... Ms. Sue Baroo
Ms. Bishie .... Ms. Mitzi Bishie

ON A YACHT

Mr. Ahoy .... Mr. Chip Ahoy
Mr. Siders .... Mr. "Doc" Siders
Ms. Korzaway .... Ms. Ann Korzaway
Mr. Monfishing .... Mr. Sal Monfishing
Mr. Toryatsee .... Mr. Vic Toryatsee
Mr. Zankor .... Mr. Ray Zankor
Mr. Kull .... Mr. Barney Kull
Mr. Sayvor .... Mr. Leif Sayvor
Ms. Tayshundeevice .... Ms. Flo Tayshundeevice

AT A GOLF TOURNAMENT

Mr. Openn .... Mr. Hugh S. Openn
Mr. Zarmee .... Mr. Arnee Zarmee
Mr. Iron .... Mr. Juan Iron
Mr. Dahohl .... Mr. Bertie Dahohl
Mr. Putt .... Mr. Juan Putt
Ms. Putt .... Ms. Meta Putt
Ms. Daparr .... Ms. Mae Daparr

Mr. Inwan	Mr. Hal Inwan
Ms. Daneegal	Ms. Mae Daneegal
Ms. Enpaarr	Ms. Eve Enparr
Ms. Birdie	Ms. Meta Birdie
Mr. Fishelroolsovgolf	Mr. Theo Fishelroolsovgolf
Mr. Kapp	Mr. Andy Kapp
Ms. Meibaggs	Ms. Carrie Meibaggs
Mr. Shott	Mr. Chip Shott
Mr. Indaruff	Mr. Hugh R. Indaruff
Mr. Stitlefft	Mr. Sly Stitlefft
Mr. Geedahole	Mr. Bo Geedahole

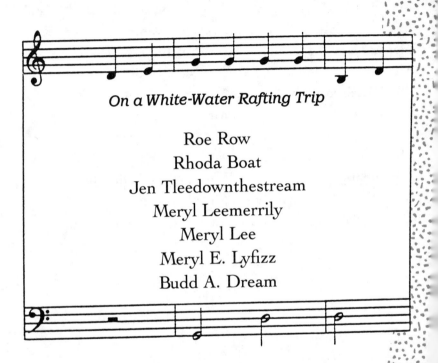

On a White-Water Rafting Trip

Roe Row
Rhoda Boat
Jen Tleedownthestream
Meryl Leemerrily
Meryl Lee
Meryl E. Lyfizz
Budd A. Dream

16 Paging:

Ms. Entsinhistoree . . .
Ms. Eve Entsinhistoree

People Likely to Be Paged:

DURING THE REVOLUTIONARY WAR

Mr. Eeze	Mr. Collin Eeze
Ms. Erteeyordeth	Ms. Lib Erteeyordeth
Mr. Coats	Mr. Redd Coats
Ms. Partee	Ms. Tory Partee
Mr. Tonteepartee	Mr. Boz Tonteepartee

DURING THE CIVIL WAR

Ms. Lishunist .... Ms. Abby Lishunist
Ms. Slaves .... Ms. Freeda Slaves
Ms. Sondicksonline .... Ms. Mae Sondicksonline
Ms. Warr .... Ms. Sybil Warr
Ms. Suppayshun .... Ms. Iman Suppayshun
Mr. Pomatticks .... Mr. Al Pomatticks
Ms. Bellum .... Ms. Ann T. Bellum

AT JOHN WAYNE BOBBITT'S HOUSE

Mr. Ernyff .... Mr. Butch Ernyff
Mr. Hertz .... Mr. Dick Hertz
Mr. S'doff .... Mr. Sly S'doff
Ms. Trayshun .... Ms. Cass Trayshun
Ms. Ball .... Ms. Dee Ball
Ms. Nissenvee .... Ms. Pia Nissenvee
Mr. Inthewoods .... Mr. Luke Inthewoods
Mr. Rosurgery .... Mr. Mike Rosurgery
Ms. Tatch .... Ms. Rhea Tatch

AT OTHER GREAT EVENTS THROUGHOUT HISTORY

Mr. Midd .... Mr. Piri Midd

Ms. Aryanz .... Ms. Barb Aryanz

Ms. Woodforrest .... Ms. Cher Woodforrest

Ms. Menn .... Ms. Mary Menn

Mr. Manempire .... Mr. Otto Manempire

Ms. Playg .... Ms. Dee Playg

Ms. Meetcake .... Ms. Letta Meetcake

Mr. Zeeanaperchiss .... Mr. Louie Zeeanaperchiss

Mr. Ammo .... Mr. Al Ammo

Ms. Bigghorn .... Ms. Lil Bigghorn

Mr. Aggofyre .... Mr. Chick Aggofyre

Ms. Rush .... Ms. Golda Rush

Mr. Erwarr .... Mr. Bo Erwarr

Mr. Tannick .... Mr. Ty Tannick

Mr. Armee .... Mr. Redd Armee

Ms. Harbor .... Ms. Pearl Harbor

Ms. Kost .... Ms. Holly Kost

Mr. Invayzhun .... Mr. Norman D. Invayzhun

Mr. O'Vackseen .... Mr. Paulie O'Vackseen

Ms. Wahl .... Ms. Beryl Lynn Wahl

Mr. Offensive .... Mr. Ted Offensive

Mr. Ergaytt .... Mr. Ward Ergaytt

Mr. Ayshun .... Mr. Ari N. Ayshun

Mr. Stroyka .... Mr. Perry Stroyka

Ms. Geddon .... Ms. Irma Geddon

17 Paging:
Ms. Otherworld . . .
Ms. Dee Otherworld

People Likely to Be Paged:

IN A CHURCH, SYNAGOGUE, OR MOSQUE

Ms. Leever	Ms. Bea Leever
Mr. Chinn	Mr. Chris Chinn
Ms. Lick	Ms. Cathy Lick
Ms. Tist	Ms. Bab Tist
Ms. Izzem	Ms. Judy Izzem
Ms. Tile	Ms. Jen Tile

Ms. Scapallion .... Ms. Eppie Scapallion

Mr. Rinn .... Mr. Luther Rinn

Mr. Lojen .... Mr. Theo Lojen

Ms. Erthanthou .... Ms. Holly Erthanthou

Ms. Preembeing .... Ms. Sue Preembeing

Mr. Syah .... Mr. Moe Syah

Ms. Sterr .... Ms. Minnie Sterr

Ms. Lama .... Ms. Dolly Lama

Mr. Jellist .... Mr. Evan Jellist

Mr. Navark .... Mr. Joe Navark

Mr. Tee .... Mr. Trini Tee

Ms. Dral .... Ms. Cathy Dral

Mr. Icka .... Mr. Basil Icka

Mr. Minsterabby .... Mr. Wes Minsterabby

Ms. O'Siss .... Ms. Di O'Siss

Ms. Sypull .... Ms. Dee Sypull

Ms. Vout .... Ms. Dee Vout

Ms. Vine .... Ms. Dee Vine

Ms. Tialbliss .... Ms. Celeste Tialbliss

Mr. Innity	Mr. Dave Innity
Ms. Noaspershuns	Ms. Cass Noaspershuns
Mr. Festation	Mr. Manny Festation
Ms. Ointed	Ms. Anne Ointed
Mr. Enning	Mr. Chris Enning
Mr. Dickshun	Mr. Benny Dickshun
Ms. Pent	Ms. Rhea Pent
Mr. Anpray	Mr. Neil Anpray
Ms. Ufleckshun	Ms. Jen Ufleckshun
Mr. Empshun	Mr. Reed Empshun
Mr. Vayshun	Mr. Sal Vayshun
Ms. Water	Ms. Hollie Water
Ms. Arreebeads	Ms. Rose Arreebeads
Ms. Zingrace	Ms. A. May Zingrace
Ms. Lewjah	Ms. Hallie Lewjah
Mr. Mary	Mr. Hale Mary
Ms. Furr	Ms. Lucy Furr
Ms. Culpa	Ms. Mia Culpa

AT A SEANCE

Ms. Voyant	Ms. Clair Voyant
Mr. Kick	Mr. Sy Kick
Mr. Board	Mr. Luigi Board
Mr. Yorcardz	Mr. Reed Yorcardz
Ms. Yorpalm	Ms. Rita Yorplam
Ms. Careful	Ms. Bess B. Careful
Ms. Ware	Ms. Bea Ware
Mr. Zadead	Mr. Ray Zadead

18 Phil Indablanx

Provide the missing first name of a person paged at:

1. a chef's convention:
   "Ms. Tedchicken . . . Ms. _____ Tedchicken."

2. a jazz concert:
   "Ms. Deblues . . . Ms. _____ Deblues"

3. the Florida Everglades:
   "Ms. Gayter . . . Ms. _____ Gayter."

4. the Museum of Natural History:
   "Mr. Dacktill . . . Mr. _____ Dacktill."

5. a political demonstration:
   "Ms. Disobedience . . . Ms. _____ Disobedience."

6. a Beckett symposium:
   "Mr. Ingforgodot . . . Mr. _____Ingforgodot."

7. a pornographic film festival:
   "Ms. Lingus . . . Ms. _____ Lingus."

8. a health club:
   "Mr. Upps . . . Mr. _____ Upps."

9. a comedy festival:
   "Mr. Murr . . . Mr. _____ Murr."

10. a wine tasting:
    "Mr. Jollay . . . Mr. _____ Jollay."

ANSWERS:

1. Rose 2. Bertha 3. Allie 4. Terry 5. Sybil 6. Wade
7. Connie 8. Sid 9. Hugh 10. Beau

19 Paging:

Mr. Indafamillee . . .
Mr. Al Indafamillee

People Likely to Be Paged:

AT ANYBODY'S MOTHER'S HOUSE

Ms. Binn .... Ms. Vera U. Binn

Mr. Upstrait .... Mr. Sid Upstrait

Ms. Knice .... Ms. Mae Knice

Ms. Kmeeproud .... Ms. Mae Kmeeproud

Ms. Pullinchinaarstarving .. Ms. Pia Pullinchinaarstarving

Mr. Watchyoodid .... Mr. Luke Watchyoodid

Mr. Happynow .... Mr. R. Hugh Happynow
Mr. Goblind .... Mr. Ewell Goblind
Mr. Mywords .... Mr. Mark Mywords
Mr. Sorry .... Mr. Ewell B. Sorry

AT A BAR MITZVAH

Mr. Iamamann .... Mr. Ted A. Iamamann

AT A WEDDING

Ms. Overheels .... Ms. Hedda Overheels
Ms. Reeyide .... Ms. Starr Reeyide
Mr. Holding .... Mr. Hans Holding
Mr. Marimee .... Mr. Will U. Marimee
Ms. Terrer .... Ms. Kay Terrer
Ms. Mann .... Ms. Bess Mann
Ms. Tronofhonor .... Ms. Mae Tronofhonor
Mr. Dissring .... Mr. Whit Dissring
Mr. Ittee .... Mr. Fidel Ittee
Ms. Sepshunline .... Ms. Rhea Sepshunline

Mr. Kaye .... Mr. Bo Kaye
Mr. Swithyourant .... Mr. Dan Swithyourant

AT A PICNIC

Mr. Dafire .... Mr. Bill Dafire
Ms. Kew .... Ms. Barb E. Kew
Mr. Berger .... Mr. Ham Berger
Mr. Slaw .... Mr. Cole Slaw
Mr. Dafood .... Mr. Bern Dafood
Ms. Sting .... Ms. Bea Sting
Ms. O'Nayze .... Ms. Mae O'Nayze
Ms. Till .... Ms. Ann Till
Ms. Indabushes .... Ms. Pia Indabushes

AT A TWINS' CONVENTION

The Hands .... Delta and Lynda
The Gants .... Ellie and Ari
The Sters .... Minnie and Barrie
The Grams .... Angie and Telly

The Lees .... Meryl and Frank
The Ings .... Josh and Sue
The Manders .... Sally and Gerry
The Rhees .... Jewel and Victor
The O'Teens .... Nick and Gil
The Smens .... Lon and Mark
The Ooshuns .... Paul and Sal
The Agayshuns .... Del and Al
The Toriums .... Audie and Maury

AT A FUNERAL

Ms. Lasswrights .... Mr. Sada Lasswrights
Mr. Tishun .... Mr. Mort Tishun
Mr. Lawn .... Mr. Forrest Lawn
Mr. Alplot .... Mr. Berry Alplot
Ms. Kett .... Ms. Cass Kett
Mr. Bearer .... Mr. Paul Bearer
Mr. Logee .... Mr. Hugh Logee
Ms. Gates .... Ms. Pearl E. Gates

Mr. Erchiff .... Mr. Hank Erchiff
Mr. Tinpiece .... Mr. Wes Tinpiece
Mr. Vederchee .... Mr. Ari Vederchee
Ms. Dalive .... Ms. Berry Dalive

20 Paging:

Mr. Ibuster . . . Mr. Phil Ibuster

People Likely to Be Paged:

AT 1600 PENNSYLVANIA AVENUE

Mr. House	Mr. Wyatt House
Ms. Garden	Ms. Rose Garden
Mr. Twing	Mr. Wes Twing
Ms. Kahnbedrum	Ms. Lynn Kahnbedrum
Ms. Fingrum	Ms. Bree Fingrum
Ms. State	Ms. Hedda State
Mr. Stopsear	Mr. Buck Stopsear

Mr. Jettdeffisitt .... Mr. Bud Jettdeffisitt

Mr. Nabill .... Mr. Sy Nabill

Mr. Power .... Mr. Vito Power

Mr. Ergate .... Mr. Ward Ergate

AT CITY HALL

Ms. Yoralcampaign .... Ms. Mae Yoralcampaign

Mr. Derman .... Mr. Al Derman

Ms. Servant .... Ms. Sybil Servant

21 Paging:
Ms. Fovahyerhedd . . .
Ms. Rue Fovahyerhedd

People Likely to Be Paged:

IN THE GARDEN

Mr. Garden .... Mr. Victor E. Garden

Mr. Spot .... Mr. Sonny Spot

Mr. Manure .... Mr. Horst Manure

Ms. Gold .... Ms. Mary Gold

Mr. D'Lion .... Mr. Dan D'Lion

Mr. Anthamum .... Mr. Chris Anthamum
Mr. Quill .... Mr. John Quill
Mr. Winkle .... Mr. Perry Winkle
Mr. Biscus .... Mr. Hy Biscus
Mr. Asinth .... Mr. Hy Asinth
Mr. Runk .... Mr. Treat Runk
Mr. Cleaves .... Mr. Ray Cleaves

AT A CONSTRUCTION SITE

Mr. Dingblock .... Mr. Bill Dingblock
Ms. Gatedsteel .... Ms. Cora Gatedsteel
Mr. Hammer .... Mr. Jack Hammer
Ms. Frame .... Ms. Dora Frame
Ms. Boards .... Ms. Flora Boards
Mr. Verdorr .... Mr. Lou Verdorr
Ms. Drillsealing .... Ms. Cathy Drillsealing
Ms. Vaytor .... Ms. Ellie Vaytor
Mr. Keefawcett .... Mr. Lee Keefawcett
Mr. Pipes .... Mr. Rusty Pipes

AT A HOME FURNISHING CENTER

Mr. Icher	Mr. Fern Icher
Mr. Drawers	Mr. Chester Drawers
Mr. Enndale	Mr. Chip Enndale
Ms. Ingroom	Mrs. Liv Ingroom
Mr. Wallcarpeting	Mr. Walter Wallcarpeting
Mr. Arugg	Mr. Ari Arugg
Mr. Doe	Mr. Wynn Doe
Mr. Enns	Mr. Kurt Enns
Mr. Doeshade	Mr. Wynn Doeshade
Mr. Shunblinds	Mr. Vinnie Shunblinds
Ms. Ningroom	Ms. Di Ningroom
Mr. D'Lear	Mr. Chan D'Lear
Ms. Verware	Ms. Syl Verware
Mr. Chentable	Mr. Kit Chentable
Mr. Urblock	Mr. Butch Urblock
Ms. Oleum	Ms. Lynn Oleum
Mr. Cherself	Mr. Dewey Cherself
Ms. Ingfan	Ms. Ceil Ingfan
Mr. Estliting	Mr. Reese Estliting
Mr. Mann	Mr. Otto Mann

22 Paging:
Mr. Finance . . .
Mr. Hy Finance

People Likely to Be Paged:

AT AN ACCOUNTANT'S OFFICE

Mr. Orrower .... Mr. Abe Orrower
Ms. Lenderbee .... Ms. Nora Lenderbee
Ms. Wise .... Ms. Penny Wise
Ms. Poundfoolish .... Ms. Ann Poundfoolish
Mr. Jett .... Mr. Bud Jett
Mr. Munny .... Mr. Xavier Munny
Mr. Treesum .... Mr. Paul Treesum

Mr. Meelater .... Mr. Bill Meelater

Ms. Over .... Ms. Carrie Over

Mr. Laytor .... Mr. Cal Q. Laytor

Ms. Fifteenth .... Ms. April Fifteenth

Mr. Tacks .... Mr. Whit Holden Tacks

Ms. Duckshin .... Ms. Dee Duckshin

Ms. Pendent .... Ms. Dee Pendent

Mr. Terr .... Mr. Shel Terr

AT THE OFFICE

Ms. Jobb .... Ms. Anita Jobb

Mr. Hyred .... Mr. Hugh R. Hyred

Mr. Fired .... Mr. Hugh R. Fired

Mr. Jerr .... Mr. Manny Jerr

Mr. Tayshun .... Mr. Dick Tayshun

Mr. Tafone .... Mr. Dick Tafone

Mr. Dexx .... Mr. Rollo Dexx

Mr. Fone .... Mr. Telly Fone

Mr. Priter .... Mr. Ty Priter

Mr. Errkooler .... Mr. Ward Errkooler

Mr. Manresorsez .... Mr. Hugh Manresorsez

Ms. Ployee .... Ms. Em Ployee

Ms. Raze .... Ms. Anita Raze

Ms. Kayshun .... Ms. Fay Kayshun

Ms. Tillattraction .... Ms. Faye Tillattraction

AT THE BANK

Mr. Donline .... Mr. Stan Donline

Mr. Nackount .... Mr. Shecky Nackount

Ms. Pozzit .... Ms. Dee Pozzit

Ms. Kahdeposit .... Ms. May Kahdeposit

Mr. Krobber .... Mr. Ben Krobber

Mr. Drawl .... Mr. Whit Drawl

Ms. Suffishentfunz .... Ms. Ann Suffishentfunz

Mr. Gage .... Mr. Moe Gage

Mr. Dentlone .... Mr. Stu Dentlone

Mr. Ding .... Mr. Len Ding

Mr. Matickteller .... Mr. Audie Matickteller

AT THE STOCK EXCHANGE

Ms. Exchange	....	Ms. Flora D. Exchange
Ms. Inn	....	Ms. Marge Inn
Ms. Holder	....	Ms. Cher Holder
Mr. Eragedbuyout	....	Mr. Lev Eragedbuyout
Mr. Etkrash	....	Mr. Mark Etkrash
Mr. Hybylow	....	Mr. Sal Hybylow
Ms. Cee	....	Ms. Essie Cee

AT IBM

Ms. Abyte	....	Ms. Meg Abyte
Mr. Dem	....	Mr. Moe Dem
Ms. Memory	....	Ms. Maura Memory
Mr. Percard	....	Mr. Hy Percard
Mr. Zerfrendlee	....	Mr. Hugh Zerfrendlee
Ms. Essdoss	....	Ms. Em Essdoss
Mr. Processor	....	Mr. Ward Processor
Mr. Rosofft	....	Mr. Mike Rosofft
Mr. Doze	....	Mr. Wynn Doze

23 Paging:

Mr. Gedthere . . .
Mr. Ewell Gedthere

People Likely to Be Paged:

IN THE AIRPORT LOUNGE

Ms. Parture	Ms. Dee Parture
Ms. Ayex	Ms. Elle Ayex
Ms. Persaver	Ms. Sue Persaver
Ms. Onlugidge	Ms. Carrie Onlugidge
Mr. Adee	Mr. Ken Adee
Mr. Syurlugidge	Mr. Lou Syurlugidge

IN THE INTERNATIONAL AIRLINES TERMINAL

Mr. Eeno	Mr. Phillip Eeno
Mr. Carlo	Mr. Monty Carlo
Ms. Jumm	Ms. Belle Jumm
Mr. Vah	Mr. Gene E. Vah
Ms. Sinkee	Ms. Elle Sinkee
Mr. Slaveeya	Mr. Hugo Slaveeya
Mr. Hannisburg	Mr. Joe Hannisburg
Mr. Rocco	Mr. Moe Rocco
Ms. Aydose	Ms. Barb Aydose
Mr. Dayjennaro	Mr. Ray O. Dayjennaro
Mr. Yah	Mr. Ken Yah
Mr. Wah	Mr. Otto Wah
Ms. Kesh	Ms. Mara Kesh
Mr. Syurlugidge	Mr. Lou Syurlugidge

IN THE DOMESTIC AIRLINES TERMINAL

Mr. Fornya	Mr. Cal E. Fornya
Mr. Tuckee	Mr. Ken Tuckee

Ms. Yaygo .... Ms. Sandy Yaygo
The Sotas .... Sara and Minne Sota
Ms. Ware .... Ms. Della Ware
Ms. Troit .... Ms. Dee Troit
Mr. Again .... Mr. Mitch Again
Mr. Abama .... Mr. Al Abama
Mr. Yammi .... Ms. Mai Yammi
Ms. Reeda .... Ms. Flo Reeda
Mr. Buhkurkee .... Mr. Al Buhkurkee
Mr. Eezianna .... Mr. Lou Eezianna
Mr. Zona .... Mr. Ari Zona
Mr. Syurlugidge .... Mr. Lou Syurlugidge

ON THE EIFFEL TOWER

Mademoiselle Voofransay ... Mademoiselle Polly Voofransay
Monsieur Voozemme .... Monsieur Jay Voozemme
Monsieur Boose .... Monsieur Otto Boose
Monsieur Mart .... Monsieur Moe Mart
Monsieur & Madame Vrah ... Lou & Lee Vrah

Monsieur Sewn .... Monsieur Gar Sewn
Mademoiselle Koo .... Mademoiselle Bo Koo
Mademoiselle Bokoo .... Mademoiselle Mercy Bokoo

IN A BEER HALL IN ARGENTINA

Mr. Toppo .... Mr. Gus Toppo
Mr. Derrhozen .... Mr. Lee Derhozen
Mr. Steppin .... Mr. Hy Steppin
Ms. Dwyer .... Ms. Barb Dwyer
Ms. Zeeyurpapers .... Ms. May I. Zeeyurpapers
Mr. Hitler .... Mr. Hy L. Hitler

AT A FOREIGN MONEY EXCHANGE

Ms. Bull .... Ms. Rue Bull
Ms. Pee .... Ms. Rue Pee
Ms. Nar .... Ms. Dee Nar
Mr. Rah .... Mr. Lee Rah

IN THE CATSKILLS

Mr. Ennsoup	Mr. Chick Ennsoup
Mr. Ennfat	Mr. Chick Ennfat
Mr. Mydawter	Mr. Meade Mydawter
Ms. Ismeer	Ms. Faye Ismeer
Mr. Abiggboy	Mr. Meyer Abiggboy
Ms. Vinn	Ms. May Vinn
Mr. Terkocker	Mr. Al Terkocker
Mr. Kess	Mr. Bub Kess
Ms. Gehleh	Ms. Fay Gehleh
Mr. Zbahyou	Mr. Howe Zbahyou

AT A SERVICE STATION

Mr. Errup	Mr. Phil Errup
Ms. Freeze	Ms. Ann T. Freeze
Ms. Fogger	Ms. Dee Fogger
Ms. Froster	Ms. Dee Froster
Mr. Mobile	Mr. Otto Mobile
Mr. Octane	Mr. Hy Octane
Ms. Lerr	Ms. Muffy Lerr
Mr. Grease	Mr. Axel Grease

THE
BATES MOTEL
REGISTRY

LEW NAHTICK

Mendel Leon Balanced

Lou Neebin

Rae Vingmadd

Ray Vinglewnahtick

Dee Ranged

Belle Vue

Lou Zyourmind

Lou Nee

Thoz O'Zine

Hy Pocondiriac

THE
BATES MOTEL
REGISTRY

Sy Koh

Klaus Trofoebick

Hal Oosinate

Dee Looshunal

Raven Madd

Perry Noid

Sy Kottick

Hy Drofoebick

Anita Shower

Thad Sallfolks